Trumpet 2 in B-flat

CHRISTMAS BRASS QUA

Two Trumpets in B-flat and Two Trombones

intermediate level

CANADIAN BRASS

ISBN 978-1-70517-575-0

EXCLUSIVELY DISTRIBUTED BY

www.canadianbrass.com
www.halleonard.com

World headquarters, contact:
Hal Leonard
7777 West Bluemound Road
Milwaukee, WI 53213
Email: info@halleonard.com

In Europe, contact:
Hal Leonard Europe Limited
1 Red Place
London, W1K 6PL
Email: info@halleonardeurope.com

In Australia, contact:
Hal Leonard Australia Pty. Ltd.
4 Lentara Court
Cheltenham, Victoria, 3192 Australia
Email: info@halleonard.com.au

CONTENTS

ANGELS WE HAVE HEARD ON HIGH

Traditional French Carol

DING, DONG! MERRILY ON HIGH

Traditional French Carol

THE FIRST NOEL

17th Century English Carol
Music from W. Sandys' *Christmas Carols*

GO, TELL IT ON THE MOUNTAIN

African-American Spiritual

GOD REST YE MERRY, GENTLEMEN

Traditional English Carol

HARK! THE HERALD ANGELS SING

Music by Felix Mendelssohn-Bartholdy

IN DULCI JUBILO

14th Century German Melody

JOY TO THE WORLD

Music by George Frideric Handel